# MORE THAN ORDINARY
# *challenges:*
### dealing with the unexpected

KIT AND DREW COONS

**More Than Ordinary Challenges: Dealing with the Unexpected**

© 2018 Kit and Drew Coons

ISBN: 978-0-9995689-3-4

All rights reserved. No part of this publication may be reproduced or transmitted in any form or by any means, electronic, mechanical, including photocopy, recording, or any information storage and retrieval system, without permission from the publisher. Requests for permission to make copies of any part of this publication should be sent to: https://morethanordinarylives.com/

Unless otherwise noted, all Scripture quotations are taken from the New American Standard Bible (NASB). Copyright © 1960, 1962, 1963, 1968, 1971, 1972, 1973, 1975, 1977, 1995 by The Lockman Foundation

Edited by Jayna Richardson
Design: Julie Sullivan (MerakiLifeDesigns.com)

First Edition

Printed in the United States

22 21 20 19 18    1 2 3 4 5

# contents

**Life's Not Fair** ............................................. 1

**The Pain is Real** ........................................... 5
   Pressure Points When Dealing with a Challenge
   Giving Up on Your Dream
   Second Guessing Yourself

**Unfortunate Responses** ............................... 15
   Making the Situation Worse
   Inflicting Suffering on Yourself
      Guilt or Shame
      Obsessing about the Future
      Anger, Bitterness, and Depression
   Inflicting Suffering on Each Other
      Blame
      Conflict
      Withdrawal
   Doubting God

**Lives Well Lived** ........................................ 33
   Discovering a God-Given Purpose
      Others Need You
   Finding Joy
      Reshaping Your Goals
      Remembering God's Past Blessings
      A Great Relationship
      Liking and Loving People
      Furry Friends

**Moving Forward** ........................................ 47
   The Desire of Your Heart
   Being Proud of the Way You Handled This
   Redeeming the Years

# LIFE'S NOT *fair*

"I never expected this to happen to me," said the former housewife in her late fifties. Her husband had left her without any money or a source of income. She struggled to make a living on a low-pay hourly job in an unfair situation.

> Drew: My mother might have said the same thing. A drunk driver had killed my father leaving her to raise three young children alone. She considered the circumstances unfair.

An old joke quotes an elderly man who had been asked his favorite Bible verse. His answer was, "It came to pass." When asked for elaboration the man explained, "Trouble came to pass. It didn't come to stay." Unfortunately, some challenges in this life do not pass quickly. They come to stay at least for an extended period. Frequently they are not fair.

*Because of the surpassing greatness of the revelations, for this reason, to keep me from exalting myself, there was given me a thorn in the flesh, a messenger of Satan to torment me—to keep me from exalting myself! Concerning this I implored the Lord three times that it might leave me. (2 Corinthians 12:7-8)*

Apostle Paul went through many hardships to fulfill his calling. In addition to the brutal hardships he endured listed in 2 Corinthians 11:24-27, he suffered an ongoing "thorn in the flesh." This challenge, presumably an eye affliction, God chose not to remove despite Paul asking three times. Some hardships God does not remove. This mini-book is about dealing with challenges which come unexpectedly and stay, perhaps for the remainder of a lifetime. Paul concluded:

*And He has said to me, "My grace is sufficient for you, for power is perfected in weakness." Most gladly, therefore, I will rather boast about my weaknesses, so that the power of Christ may dwell in me. (2 Corinthians 12:9)*

"I hope someday," our parents told us, "that you have children just like you!" This mild form of parental revenge gave them a small measure of satisfaction in their frustration at our behavior. Someday, justice would be done. Had we thought about it, we might have agreed: "I hope that my children will be like me." Perhaps we would have added, "Except with more opportunities than I was given." Certainly we assumed that we would have children.

However, life for some doesn't turn out that way, and yet within nearly all of us is the desire to leave part of ourselves behind. We desire a somebody like us, only better, to see a future that we will not. This desire to nurture and teach a child by birth or adoption is a God-given instinct. Fulfilling instincts is a basic human need that, when denied, causes emotional turmoil. In our case, we spent seven years in infertility treatments and on adoption waiting lists. Through that ordeal, God taught us how to deal with an unfixable challenge.

This mini-book uses our situation of childlessness as an example. However, many other challenges can have the same emotional effect. Consider someone who longs for a loving spouse, but doesn't have one. Or someone who has lost a spouse by death or divorce. What about parents with a prodigal child who, despite receiving an ocean of love, discipline, and prayers, insists on making ruinous choices? Perhaps others struggle with a disability or illness that limits their dreams. Maybe parents have lost their only child in a tragic accident. Some have been left alone through circumstances beyond their control. All of these examples are unexpected and unwelcome life challenges.

Many heartwarming stories share about difficult situations that worked out miraculously or through a person's iron-willed determination. The stories are useful in that they inspire hope. But sometimes life just doesn't work out that way. What do we do in a situation that seems unfair?

The answer is that we must trust God to help us look past the unfairness. Then we need to make good choices about what to do with our lives.

> Every moment separates our lives into before and after. Some moments divide our lives into never before and always after. Many of those life-changing moments

are based on the choices we make. God allows us to make choices through free will. Most awake moments include minor decisions. Some decisions are more consequential and will affect the remainder of our lives. Making good choices at those moments is for our good and ultimately reflect on God as we represent Him in this world.[1] (*Coons, More Than Ordinary Choices*)

Especially when facing major life challenges, making the choices carefully with the best possible biblical principles is imperative. Since many have unexpected challenges, we have specifically designed this material to be easily adapted to a Bible study using discussion questions. If studying as a couple, individual, or group, please take time to think through your responses to the questions after each section.

### Questions for Thought

What are some examples of seemingly unchangeable situations than can challenge us?

Do you have an unexpected situation that is challenging? Will you tell the group about it?

Does your situation seem fair? If not, how does that make you feel?

# THE PAIN IS
## *real*

---

"We're praying for you to have children," well-wishers promised. Then many added, "You would make such wonderful parents." Meanwhile, we tried every infertility treatment available and waited on an adoption list. Yet year after year went by, and our arms remained empty. Every painful month felt like losing another baby.

> Kit: I can remember it as if it were yesterday. For everyone else, it was a day just like any other. For me, it was a day that changed my life. We had just failed at our last attempt at an in-vitro procedure. We drove home in silence. Our home had always been a source of comfort to me, but the sight of it brought no reassurance that day. I found myself pacing around

*each room and then the yard, but I couldn't find anywhere to hide. At that point, I didn't want life to continue, so I went to the closet, crawled in, and closed the door. Maybe if I just hid long enough, it would all go away.*

Our decades-ago dream of having children never materialized. Many going through this or some other heartbreaking circumstance have asked, "How do you survive? How do you make the pain go away? When do you give up on your dream?" We share our story with you in the hope that you will be encouraged in the unique journey God has given you. Our prayer is that you will appreciate our frankness, learn about dealing with pain, and consider the character of God as you apply lessons we learned to your own specific situation.

### **Questions for Thought**

What are some unhealthy emotions an unexpected challenge might cause?



Have you found ways to deal with unhealthy emotions?

How can the pain of an unexpected challenge affect a person on a long-term basis?

## *Pressure Points When Dealing with a Challenge*

Ethical decisions added to our trauma in seeking a child. A physician actually prescribed pornography, which Drew declined, to ensure a good semen sample during our fertility treatments. Scientifically viable methods, such as a sperm donor or the use of a surrogate mother, were options. The emotional price such choices required could undermine any marriage. In-vitro fertilization brought the possibility of difficult choices regarding disposal of unused eggs or zygotes. Adoption brought its own set of difficult questions and ethicalities. Would we accept a special-needs child? Did we want a baby of another race or nationality? You may find that you and your spouse have very different values regarding the choices you face.

The uncertainty of your situation and future may cause great stress. We struggled with decisions about how far to go medically and with the adoption process. We clearly remember feeling unfairness. Why couldn't we be like everyone else? Just the reality of having to ask these questions made us angry, let alone trying to answer them. Most couples we knew had little to worry about beyond deciding what color they were going to paint the nursery.

Uncertainty of not being sure how to plan your lives complicates your thinking. *Should we convert that third bedroom into an office or save it for a nursery? Should we buy a house in this town?* We also endured the uncertainty of *Who will carry on my name?* In our case, both of us had third-generation names we had wished to pass on to our children. Then there was the question of *Will we let our families down if we don't have children?* Unfortunately, many families are quick to voice their insensitive opinion that you will disappoint them if you don't have children.

In our case, the expenses of medical treatments also added stress. Couples who pursue either natural birth or adoption usually have major financial decisions to make; either process can be very expensive. Financial issues are the most frequent cause of fights among couples. Financial values and priorities are inevitably different between spouses. Two individuals' propensity for risk-taking may also come into conflict. Are you willing to spend $20,000 on a treatment that may have only a 10% chance of success? Are you willing to mortgage your home and work a second job to adopt a special-needs baby? Some are. Others are not.

Another pressure point may be timing. While trying to have children, we certainly experienced time pressure. Everyone agrees that no one is getting any younger. Kit felt her biological clock ticking during our infertility process. What to do and when to do it are decisions that add additional pressure on couples. All these issues, and many others, are extraordinary challenges.

We will not attempt to define your values for you. And your challenge is likely different from ours. However, we do encourage you to make choices based on scriptural principles. In most relationships, one of the spouses is more persuasive. In other cases, one spouse, possibly the husband, is completely authoritative. In making ethically difficult decisions, you must each—especially the one who is most persuasive or authoritative—be extra sensitive to the other's feelings and values. The goal is to reach decisions together, even if that means moving very slowly.

**Questions for Thought**

What pressure points have you experienced in a difficult situation?




How did you deal with them?

Why do pressure points make dealing with a challenge more difficult?

## *Giving Up on Your Dream*

> *Each man has his own gift from God, one in this manner, and another in that. (1 Corinthians 7:7)*

People enduring their own disappointments still ask us, "When do you stop trying to fulfill a dream?" The medical community is constantly discovering new procedures that offer hope to a desperate heart. You always think, *Surely next time will be successful*. We had many people tell us, "God wouldn't decide not to give you children. You'd be such great parents." We even had a pastor, unsolicited by us, tell us prophetically, "I see dirty diapers in your future." Those well-meant comments, the internal desire for children, and the pressure of being different from everyone else, all compounded the pain.

We spent seven years in medical treatments and remained on the adoption list until Drew passed the recommended maximum age. We also had the issue of our medical insurance being unwilling to help with the expenses. Finally, we realized that our lives had become consumed with the pursuit of a child.

*Drew: At a Christian conference, I was searching my heart about our dilemma. I was mindful of 1 Peter 4:10, "Each of you should use whatever gift you have received to serve others." (NIV) What was our gift? Then I got a strong impression from God telling me, "Take the gift that I've given you." Could childlessness be a gift? If so, our choice was to accept God's gift or reject it. We decided to accept childlessness as a gift from God.*

Is childlessness the gift we would have chosen? No, but we believe that was the gift God had for us. Because we felt so strongly about the importance of family, we joined a Christian ministry dedicated to biblical marriage. With the freedom childlessness gave, we have been privileged to start over 450 separate Bible study groups and speak in hundreds of churches. We led over a hundred conferences and seminars all over the US plus spoke in 39 other countries. To this day, we continue to coach leaders and ministers in many of those countries. Likely thousands of children have been able to grow up with two loving parents through our gift of childlessness.

We cannot tell you when to give up your specific dream. We realistically assessed our probability of success versus the effect the effort had on our lives and service to God. In that context, God gave us a new vision. We recognized our circumstances to be a unique gift from God that we could offer back to Him. To reject the gift would be to reject the Giver as well. Our Lord has used that gift more than we ever would have imagined.

## Questions for Thought

Have you ever had to give up on a dream?

How did it affect you?

Have you recognized an alternate gift God may have given to you?

## *Second Guessing Yourself*

Even though we had reconciled ourselves to God's will for our lives, the pain remained. Very caring individuals would still claim with good intentions, "God has told me that you *will* have children." The questions haunted us. Did we make the right decision? Should we have tried one more round of infertility treatments? Should we have adopted from a third-world country? Those who have given up a dream, whatever the dream may be, frequently become world-class second guessers.

In addition to the uncertainty, an underlying sadness can sometimes plague those who have unfulfilled dreams. Frequently, the sadness catches you when other disappointments enter your life and make you introspective. For example, when health or financial difficulties hit, you may find yourself overwhelmed with emotion out of proportion to the current difficulty. Even when we were happy and certain of God's will, a pang of regret came when meeting someone about the age our child could have been.

We also experienced the heartache of "sharing" the pain of infertility with other couples, seeing them get pregnant, and watching them joyously leave us behind. It seemed like they couldn't get away from us soon enough. Of course, they didn't mean to be insensitive. But circumstances like this will remind you of your grief. There is always that little prick of pain, even though you are actually very happy for others.

Every person who has been in any heart-rendering and unchangeable situation has suffered the pain of uncertainty and longing. The issue becomes *How will we respond to the pain?* There is a tremendous amount at stake. The way we respond to an unexpected life challenge impacts the entirety of our lives.

## Questions for Thought

Have you observed others second guessing themselves after a difficult decision?

What are some ways people second guess themselves?

How can second guessing be counter productive?

# UNFORTUNATE *responses*

Have you ever accidentally hit your thumb with a hammer? Perhaps the first person who attempted to console you got a surprise. In severe pain, we often lash out at innocent bystanders or even those we love. Although the trauma of an unexpected life challenge may draw a couple together for a while, the pain is almost certain to make you lash out unintentionally. Certainly, that degree of stress can make even the most pleasant person irritable.

Suffering from heartbreak, individuals may unconsciously punish themselves or even look for unrelated faults in others, likely their spouse. This displaced anger only multiplies their agony. Couples end up harming themselves and each other when they don't address the pain openly and honestly.

## *Making the Situation Worse*

People in pain often go to unusual or even ill-conceived methods to relieve their suffering. Scripture gives an example of a difficult situation made worse by a poor decision. Fortunately for us, the example even relates to childlessness. But the principle of not overreacting in a difficulty applies to any challenge. In Genesis, God promised Abram (later renamed Abraham) that his descendants would be a great nation. This was a significant promise, but one that required waiting.

> *Now Sarai, Abram's wife had borne him no children, and she had an Egyptian maid whose name was Hagar. So Sarai said to Abram, "Now behold, the Lord has prevented me from bearing children. Please go in to my maid; perhaps I shall obtain children through her." And Abram listened to the voice of Sarai. And after Abram lived ten years in the land of Canaan, Abram's wife Sarai took Hagar the Egyptian, her maid, and gave her to her husband Abram as his wife. And he went in to Hagar, and she conceived; and when she saw that she had conceived, her mistress was despised in her sight. And Sarai said to Abram, "May the wrong done me be upon you. I gave my maid into your arms; but when she saw that she had conceived, I was despised in her sight. May the Lord judge between you and me. (Genesis 16:1-5)*

Sarai had tired of waiting and felt compelled to do something about the situation. Admittedly Abram wasn't much help. But Sarai only made things worse—worse for her, worse for Abram, and worse for Hagar. Sarai's bitter words to Abram, "May the wrong done me be upon you," illustrate both blame and conflict between spouses.

The following pages discuss subtle spiritual temptations which would make any situation worse. Lest we neglect the obvious, drug abuse, crime, immorality, gambling, and other activities outside of God's biblical instructions may seem to grant respite during a severe challenge. But any of these can destroy a life that has wonderful potential despite the challenge.

As we seek God in our challenges, we need to look at how our actions will affect ourselves and others. Are we only concerned with ending our own pain? Are we so focused on ourselves that we can't see what our actions might do to our spouse? Are we objective in decision making? These are all good questions that we need to keep in mind as we walk through times of difficulty.

## Questions for Thought

Have you ever observed anyone make a difficult situation worse through their actions?

Why do you think people do ill-advised things in a difficult situation?

# Inflicting Suffering on Yourself

*For it is better, if it is God's will, to suffer for doing good than for doing evil. (1 Peter 3:17)*

Any of us may bring unnecessary pain on ourselves or make suffering worse. Peter indicated that we can suffer for doing right or wrong and exhorts us to suffer for the right reasons. God created humans with a free will. Only that way could they experience the deepest voluntary relationship with Him. A free will requires the ability to make choices. Poor choices can lead to suffering. Were God to eliminate that suffering, then free will would not be all that God intends.[2] (Coons, *More than Ordinary Faith*)

## Guilt or Shame

Sometimes we torture ourselves with guilt. We fear past sins are preventing us from having what we desire. When an unexpected challenge enters our lives, our natural response is to think, "If only I hadn't . . ." or, "If only I had been more careful . . ." And from those questions comes the personal accusation, "God must be punishing me." This can lead to shame. Couples struggling with any challenge are acutely aware that others are observing them. A voice from Satan may whisper, "They know God is punishing you."

Do not be mistaken. Sin is a very serious matter to God. Scripture warns us that people do reap the consequences of their actions. "Do not be deceived, God is not mocked; for whatever a man sows, this he will also reap." (Galatians 6:7) However, God readily extends forgiveness to all who repent. 1 John 1:9 promises, "If we confess our sins, he is faithful and just to forgive us of our sins and to cleanse us from all unrighteousness." Therefore, if you have repented of past sins, there is no basis for torturing yourself about previous mistakes.

Some may misinterpret Exodus 34:7, "He will by no means leave the guilty unpunished, visiting the iniquity of fathers on the children and on the grandchildren to the third and fourth generations." Most Christians interpret this scripture as the descendants having learned behavior from predecessors that leads to bad consequences. But couples in the anguish of a severe challenge sometimes assume that their difficulty is God's deliberate punishment on them for the parents' or grandparents' sins. Does that sound like the God who promises to "...forgive us of our sins and to cleanse us from all unrighteousness"?

Fortunately for our personal challenge, Scripture has a point-on example of an egregious sin that resulted in severe consequences but did not affect fertility. 2 Samuel 11 reveals how David failed morally as the king of Israel. He observed Uriah's wife, Bathsheba, bathing on a neighboring roof while her husband served with the army. David sent for Bathsheba and had relations with her. Later she sent a message that she had become pregnant. Since her husband was away, his un-involvement would become obvious. Implicit was a warning that David would be revealed as the one responsible. David tried to cover up by bringing Uriah home to have relations with Bathsheba. But Uriah refused to sleep with his wife in accordance to scriptural guidelines for the army. As a result, David arranged to leave Uriah exposed on the battlefield, where he was killed. David then married Bathsheba. Then God sent Nathan the prophet to confront David.

*Then David said to Nathan, "I have sinned against the Lord." Nathan said to David, "The Lord also has taken away your sin. However, because by this deed you have given occasion to the enemies of the Lord to blaspheme, the child also that is born to you shall surely die." (2 Samuel 12:13-14)*

If ever there was ample reason to use infertility as a punishment, this was the occasion. David did not escape the consequences. The baby died. And Nathan added, "I (God) will raise evil against you from your own household." (2 Samuel 12:11) David's family was subsequently divided by his rebellious sons. But even after this sin, God did not use infertility as a punishment. After David repented, God gave David and Bathsheba another son who became King Solomon. Solomon also had many children, as did his children. They are the forbearers of Christ.

Our mini-book *More than Ordinary Faith: Why Does God Allow Suffering* reveals scriptural reasons God allows suffering. In no case is suffering alleviated by guilt or shame.

## Questions for Thought
Why do you think people have a tendency to blame themselves?

### Obsessing about the Future
We once met a couple struggling with infertility who had set up a nursery in their home. The baby bed, toys, and clothes must have been a constant reminder to them about their plight. We are only human when we dream about how our lives could have been different. But if we allow ourselves to be consumed by these thoughts, we can destroy the life that God has given us. Planning for

the future, daydreaming about what could be, and visualizing a life we don't have all inflict needless suffering.

> Kit: We all need a little time for some escape. For us, a movie can be a great way to escape. I remember one instance vividly. We got our popcorn and settled down for complete withdrawal from our challenges. The movie was enjoyable until the end. That's when the main character got a sneak peek into his future. The dream started with a beautiful home and two young children playing in the yard. At this point, I felt okay. Then the adorable wife appeared—pregnant with child number three. The perfect home, the perfect family, the dream come true. I had been trying to get a little relief from the challenge of not having children. Even Hollywood was against me. I left the theater in tears.

One of the ways to not obsess about the future is to set some boundaries. Our actions as well as our thoughts need limits. Most of us would agree that the last place we need to be when we are on a diet is in a bakery. Stopping by "just for a quick look," smelling the wonderful aromas, and maybe even enjoying a sample are not wise. For us, daydreaming about children was a lot like going into that bakery. We knew we shouldn't be doing so. Even knowing pain would follow, we frequently couldn't resist. Scripture encourages us to take control of our thoughts.

*For the weapons of our warfare are not of the flesh but are divinely powerful for the destruction of fortresses. We are destroying speculations and every lofty thing raised up against the knowledge of God, and we are taking every thought captive to the obedience of Christ. (2 Corinthians 10:4-5)*

Taking control of our thoughts might include avoiding some situations. Attending a baby shower became very difficult for Kit during our struggle. Putting herself under that incredible emotional and physical tension was neither smart nor necessary. Setting some limits for activities is okay. Don't be afraid to carry them out. Knowing what we can handle and living within those boundaries will give us time to heal.

## Questions for Thought

Have you ever struggled with thinking about what could have been or something unlikely to happen?




How did you take your thoughts captive to the obedience of Christ?




## Anger, Bitterness, and Depression

In the anguish of dealing with any unexpected life challenge, only rarely does a person not experience some degree of anger. In our case, infertility treatments were expensive, painful, de-humanizing, and always disappointing. Adoption procedures were slow, tedious, and unsuccessful. Anger resulted from the difficulty and constant reminders of our challenge. Anger, whether it be overt or suppressed, is a normal reaction. Many of us may already have difficulty with anger. Then pain intensifies the struggle.

> Drew: I learned from my father that in a disagreement, if you get angry enough, you get your way. For some of us anger is an unfortunate part of our nature. Men are particularly susceptible to anger. In our culture, if a man is very tender, compassionate, humble . . . he's a wimp. But if he gets mad . . . now there's a real man for you. Anger is one of the few culturally acceptable masculine emotions. As a result, many men learn to channel nearly all their emotions into anger. They learn to feel comfortable, perhaps even self-righteous, with anger.

During challenges, couples are likely to feel unjustly treated. They can become aggrieved, perhaps even at God. "Why can't we be like normal couples? Why us?" Anger steals our objectivity. Anger can make us overreact in other situations. Anger makes us doubt God's goodness.

> *A man's discretion makes him slow to anger. And it is his glory to overlook a transgression. (Proverbs 19:11)*

Continual suppressed anger can progress into something even more dangerous. The Bible includes another word for low-grade anger. That word is bitterness. Scripture particularly warns husbands to avoid becoming embittered against their wives. "Husbands, love your wives and do not be embittered against them." (Colossians 3:19) All of us are warned not to let a root of bitterness take hold in our lives. Bitterness will distort our perceptions of life.

> *See to it that no one comes short of the grace of God; that no root of bitterness springing up causes trouble, and by it many be defiled. (Hebrews 12:15)*

The pain of difficult circumstances over a prolonged period can result in bitterness. Once again we have a point-on example. The Bible recognizes bitterness in the context of childlessness. If anyone ever had justification to be bitter, it would be Hannah. The scorn of another woman even magnified her anguish. And yet Hannah's example teaches us in any challenge how to not allow bitterness to destroy our lives.

> *And when the day came that Elkanah sacrificed, he would give portions to Peninnah his wife and to all her sons and her daughters; but to Hannah he would give a double portion, for he loved Hannah, but the Lord had closed her womb. Her rival, however, would provoke her bitterly to irritate her, because the Lord had closed her womb. And it happened year after year, as often as she went up to the house of the Lord, she would provoke her, so she wept and would not eat. (1 Samuel 1:4-7)*

Peninnah, by her cruel remarks to Hannah, added greatly to her pain. So much so, that Hannah was not able to eat. She had good reason to be bitter—bitter that she didn't have children, bitter that she had to live with Peninnah's remarks, bitter over not living up to what her culture expected of her. Failure to eat can even be a symptom of depression, perhaps induced by suppressed anger and bitterness.

> *Now Eli the priest was sitting on the seat by the doorpost of the temple of the Lord. And she (Hannah), greatly distressed, prayed to the Lord and wept bitterly. And Hannah made a vow and said, "O Lord of Hosts, if Thou wilt indeed look on the affliction of Thy maidservant and remember me, and not forget Thy maidservant, but will give Thy maidservant a son, then I will give him to the Lord all the days of his life, and a razor shall never come on his head." Now it came about, as she continued praying before the Lord, that Eli was watching her mouth. As for Hannah, she was speaking in her heart, only her lips were moving, but her voice was not heard. So Eli thought she was drunk. Then Eli said to her, "How long will you make yourself drunk? Put away wine from you." But Hannah answered and said, "No, my Lord, I am a woman oppressed in spirit; I have drunk neither wine nor strong drink, but I have poured out my soul before the Lord." (1 Samuel 1: 9-18)*

Hannah rose early to beseech the Lord to give her a child, and then she committed that child to Him. As she exposed her heart, she was misunderstood by Eli, the priest. She explained to Eli and then left to return to her normal responsibilities. She began to eat again and her countenance changed. Hannah overcame potential bitterness.

Perhaps you've been tempted to believe that the Lord is not interested in how your heart feels. Hannah's experience tells us something very different. She went to the Lord and poured out her heart. So emotional was her plea to God, Eli thought she was drunk. She indeed told the Lord everything that was in her heart: the pain, the anguish, even the bitterness. We should do the same in our distress. As we do, our bitterness will fade and depression becomes less likely.

Not all depression is caused by suppressed anger and bitterness. But some is. We recommend *The Anger Workbook*[3] by Les Carter and Frank Minirth and *Happiness is a Lifestyle*[4] by Frank Minirith.

### Questions for Thought

Can you think of ways other than those listed a person could make the situation worse?

How could the ideas listed or identified in the previous question affect a person's life?

How can anger, bitterness, and depression ruin a person's life more than the unexpected challenge they face?

## Inflicting Suffering on Each Other

Couples can also inadvertently or even deliberately cause each other pain. Couples may not even realize that their actions are exacerbated by their struggle with the challenge besetting them.

### Blame

All of us remember that in our wedding vows we promised some version of "for better or worse." Life brings challenges that can seem like we are living in the worst. In this context, it's quite human to look for someone to blame. And who is the most convenient to blame? Our spouse. And the fault, such as a medical problem or lost job, may literally be theirs. The spouse with the "problem" is not immune to casting blame either. Most couples will not directly blame each other for their challenge. However, they often inadvertently create an environment of blame, perhaps criticizing one another for unrelated reasons.

> Kit: A principle that I've found helpful is to remind myself that my spouse is not my enemy. When we are under stress, the easiest one to blame is our spouse. Often, Drew will catch me pacing back and forth saying under my breath, "Drew is not my enemy, Drew is not my enemy." This helps change my perspective. It reminds me to not take the problem out on Drew, which would only make things worse.

Look back at Sarai's situation in Genesis 16:5: "And Sarai said to Abram, 'May the wrong done me be upon you.'" What clearer example of blaming could we have? Certainly her words made the situation worse or hampered Abram and Sarai from dealing with it.

## Conflict

"We don't even know what started the fight." This is a common lament from couples who have let a disagreement get out of control. They have then said or done things to hurt each other, which makes the situation worse. Frequently, fights occur in an environment of discontent or discouragement. Some of the most destructive fights we ever had were during the difficult years of infertility treatments. The specific topics were always something besides our infertility. However, that difficulty created an environment of extreme pressure that made us more sensitive and ready to fight.

Most healthy relationships have disagreements. With only rare exceptions, a couple who has no conflict has stopped communicating. They are dealing with their differences by pretending those differences do not exist. Or one spouse could be so dominant that the other does not express any ideas or opinions. Neither situation is healthy.

All of us would agree that communication is foundational in a successful marriage. Unfortunately, communication conducted poorly often leads to fights. We define a fight as when you say or do things to hurt each other. Physical violence is never a godly response. And verbal violence, when you say things to hurt your spouse, is just as serious. A verbal blow can take longer to heal than a bruise or even a broken bone. The early American author Washington Irving wrote that "the tongue is the only tool that gets sharper with use."[5] Proverbs 10:19 speaks powerfully when it says,

"Where there are many words, transgression is unavoidable." This is especially true when in an environment made more tense by an ongoing challenge.

> *Let no unwholesome word proceed from your mouth, but only such a word as is good for edification according to the need of the moment, so that it will give grace to those who hear. (Ephesians 4:29)*

There are many biblical resources on communicating lovingly and safely. If you are saying or doing things that hurt your spouse, those resources could be helpful. We recommend *Staying Close*[6] by Dennis Rainey.

## Withdrawal

Considering the hurt a struggling couple may inflict on each other through blame or conflict, the temptation is to protect oneself. A couple can easily drift into living separate lives at a time when they need each other the most.

> Drew: "Just don't think about it," I told Kit angrily. "Just do what you have to do!" Kit, at that time, was taking daily hormone shots and driving 250 miles a week to see our infertility doctor. She seemed obsessed with babies. I was certain that she made herself emotionally worse by talking about the situation. My solution was to pretend nothing was happening. I refused to talk about anything related to children except the essentials of what we needed to do at any given time. When she persisted, I tried to divert her attention by becoming critical in other areas. Maybe that will give her something else to think about, I superficially

*reasoned. But forcing her to keep her heart bottled up was hardly supportive. Unfortunately, only years later I realized how my reaction to Kit was an unhealthy coping response to my own pain in the situation.*

Life brings trouble. Being married means sharing it.[7]
(Coons, *More Than Ordinary Marriage*)

Trouble can do one of two things: It can draw us together, or it can drive us to opposite corners where we're likely to come out fighting. Ultimately, the ongoing fighting can lead to withdrawal from each other. God wants us instead to use the challenges in our lives to build the character of our marriages by binding our hearts together. We urge couples to learn how to biblically communicate without fighting. The mini-book *More Than Ordinary Marriage* addresses communication in the section "A Private Language."

### Questions for Thought

How could the pain of a difficult challenge make a spouse or other loved one insensitive to another's needs?

When this happens during intense pain, what should each of the parties do?

How could blame, conflict, or withdrawal in an unexpected challenge hurt a relationship?

## *Doubting God*

1 Thessalonians 5:21, which relates specifically to wisdom from God, says, "Test everything. Hold on to the good." Sincere questioning isn't the same as doubting. "Doubting Thomas" was not present when Jesus first appeared after the Resurrection. Thomas insisted that unless he could see and touch, he would not believe. Eight days later, Jesus reappeared with Thomas present. When Thomas professed belief, Jesus mildly rebuked him for not believing previously. Testing truth by expecting evidence was not Thomas's shortfall. Evidence had already been provided by the empty tomb and the eyewitness testimonies. Thomas's mistake was demanding absolute proof.

However, any severe challenge is a form of suffering, which can lead to doubt of God's character and love for us.

> Why does God allow suffering? This is a universal question in every culture and in every heart. And the question is reasonable and valid. Lack of a meaningful answer is a barrier to the faith of many. Shallow answers can undermine faith. Fortunately, the Bible gives clear reasons that God allows suffering.[8] (Coons, *More Than Ordinary Faith*)

*More Than Ordinary Faith* gives God's biblical purposes to answer the "why" question regarding suffering. The mini-book also explains how we can bring unnecessary suffering on ourselves. More importantly, the text gives biblical responses that can lessen suffering.

> God never wastes pain. He always uses it to accomplish His purpose. And His purpose is for His glory and our good.[9] (Heald, *Becoming a Woman of Excellence*)

### Questions for Thought

Why could suffering cause someone to doubt God?

How could doubting God make a challenge more difficult?

Could confidence that the Bible gives meaningful reasons for suffering be an antidote to doubt?

# LIVES WELL *lived*

---

One reason parenthood is wonderful is that it brings qualities such as unselfishness and self-sacrifice out of most people. We've got good news! God wants those qualities for you regardless of the challenge you face. But many are caught in limbo not knowing what to do with their lives because of their challenge. Whatever your challenge, we urge you to find a God-given purpose. God can use this purpose to bring the best out of you. We don't want to waste our lives. Each day is a gift from God.

## Discovering a God-Given Purpose

*Each of you should use whatever gift you have received to serve others, as faithful stewards of God's grace in its various forms. (1 Peter 4:10, NIV)*

Do you hate platitudes? Do overly simplistic solutions to complex problems irritate you? Perhaps the most irritating platitude would be, "When life gives you lemons, make lemonade." When people said that to us while we were in the midst of infertility, we needed to restrain ourselves from violence. Nevertheless, making the best of a difficult situation is the key to dealing with life's challenges.

All of us need meaning and purpose. Scripture warns, "Where there is no vision, the people perish." (Proverbs 29:18, KJV) In fact, the struggle for meaning and purpose often dominates people's lives. The question is, "What is really worthy of the investment of our lives?" Is the goal a career, a beautiful home, or a life filled with unique experiences? All of these are fine in themselves. Still, we would like to offer a more lasting answer. We suggest an investment of your lives that will reap eternal returns.

> Drew: "If you want to feel better about yourself, do something for someone else," my grandmother would say. She could even help you to do so by assigning some chores, if needed. I always thought the good feeling that followed was relief at being finished with the work. Perhaps there was more joy at a job done for someone else than I realized. "Get your eyes off of yourself" is a well-known axiom in dealing with nearly any emotional trauma.

Couples in the midst of a challenge may find thinking about anything else difficult. We need to be careful to not allow our lives to be dominated by that challenge. All of us need a higher God-given purpose to occupy our minds and hearts. A key part of God's purpose for each of us is to invest our lives in others.

> Kit: God began to use our willingness to serve Him by allowing us to minister to others through marriage seminars. With each new seminar, the Lord would whisper in my ear, "Kit, this is a 'child' I am giving you. Be aware of my blessing in it, enjoy each moment, and keep them in your heart." It has been a delight over the years to have been given so many "children" by the Lord. I treasure each one.

The ultimate expectation in marriage is not in our consensus that we are one, but in our commitment to something bigger than any of us.[10] (Gaither, *Christianity Today*)

## Others Need You

Regardless of the challenge you face, other people need you. Many who are home-bound or even incapacitated serve others by their prayers. All of us know stories about influential teachers whom God used to touch lives. You don't necessarily need to be a professional teacher. Nearly every church has a need for teachers and child-care workers. In our case, we had a tremendous love for children. Without having children of our own, we found we could spread our love to many children, especially by teaching their parents how to have a good relationship. We also taught children's classes in our church all the seven years we were in infertility treatments. One church we attended pulled all the eleven- and twelve-year-olds together for us to give them the "birds and bees" talk from a godly perspective. This was rather uncomfortable, but important.

> Kit: I taught Vacation Bible School for many years and enjoyed them all. But the one I'll never forget was when I surprised one of the students with a birthday cake. He amazed me with his excitement. I have always loved my own birthday celebrations. Birthday cake is right up there on the list of things I love most. But this child was overwhelmed. It was a joy to behold! He thanked me for months! What I didn't know until much later was that his home life was anything but joyful. Shortly after this celebration, his father committed suicide. What a tragedy for one so young to have to experience. I was always grateful to the Lord that He used me to bake a simple cake to give that little boy a few happy moments.

Kit had the idea of having an annual Easter egg hunt in our large yard. Can you imagine 150-200 kids with full baskets and their parents in your yard? We did that for ten years. But the most fun is the fishing pond we now have. Kids come to our house and catch a fish big enough to make their dads jealous. We were never parents, but we've been grandparents to plenty of children. We've also had time for nieces and nephews. Family members appreciate time you can spend with their children. Developing a relationship with your nieces or nephews will enrich your life and theirs. Kit's sister shared that her daughter said, "When Auntie Kit comes for a visit, it's like she brings armloads of love with her."

You bring different experiences and perspective to the child's life than their parents. And depending on the depth of the relationship, your nieces and nephews might receive meaningful advice from you more readily than from their parents. We have a unique opportunity to have an impact on the lives of those within our own extended family.

Those willing to serve others have literally an infinite number of opportunities. Visiting folks at the nursing home, baking cookies for the police or fire department, finding ways to show a pastor and church staff that you appreciate them, and opening your home to your neighbors for a local Bible study are all worthwhile.

You may be surprised how God can use what you already love doing. For example, if you love tennis, you could give lessons to underprivileged children. If you love reading, there are many home-bound or hospitalized individuals who would love hearing you read. Also, many children or adults need help learning how to read. We knew one very quiet man who loved to garden. His service to others was growing vegetables and giving them away. Many people are delighted by the gift of fresh vegetables. Another couple we knew loved animals.

They kept a whole menagerie of friendly dogs, goats, pigs, ducks, chickens, and sheep as pets. Their service was to provide a petting area for children through various charity organizations.

### Question for Thought
What are some worthwhile and fulfilling God-given purposes?

## Finding Joy

*But the fruit of the Spirit is love, joy, peace, patience, kindness, goodness, faithfulness, gentleness, self-control; against such things there is no law.*
*(Galatians 5:22-23)*

This verse demonstrates that the Holy Spirit is ready to develop these qualities in our lives. But we need to be willing and do our part seeking joy in difficult challenges so the Holy Spirit can give us all God offers. The following are some ways we have found to seek joy.

### Reshaping your Goals
Investing our lives well may require reshaping our goals. When we experience an unexpected challenge, our temptation is to think, "I'll never be happy again." One way to help ourselves move through those changes is to set new goals. As we said,

we believe that God gave us the gift of time and energy to invest in other families. That may not have been the gift we would have chosen, but it is the special gift God chose for us. We needed to be willing to faithfully employ it in serving others.

In the previous section, "Others Need You," we gave examples of services to others that can give fulfillment and joy. In dealing with a difficult challenge, setting goals of service can magnify joy by making you more effective. Our goal became to strengthen thousands of families by helping moms and dads to love each other more deeply and work effectively together as a team. Others have set goals to collect a large quantity of food for the needy or to raise sufficient money for a significant project.

*Religion that God our Father accepts as pure and faultless is this: to look after orphans and widows in their distress. (James 1:27)*

We believe that "widows and orphans" are examples of any individuals who are disadvantaged and have no way to ever repay you for your acts of kindness. According to James, you can't go wrong ministering to them. Prisoners, the disabled, or homeless individuals would also fall into the same category. Even if you take a very literal interpretation of this scripture to mean exclusively widows and orphans, there are still a multitude of opportunities. Today our culture is full of children, especially those who are fatherless, who are eager for someone to love them.

Regardless of how you interpret James 1:27, we encourage you to set goals that are large enough that you must trust God and work hard to accomplish them. Achieving them will bring you great joy. And the effort required will take your mind off the challenge that could otherwise dominate your lives.

## Remembering God's Past Blessings

When we quickly read through the Old Testament, miracles seem to have happened every day. God spoke to Abraham, gave him a new home, helped him win a war, preserved his family, gave him the long-awaited promised son, and tested his faith. All of this occurs within a few short chapters in Genesis. And yet the Scriptures record that Abraham actually lived to be 175 years old. There must have been many years when God seemed inactive. But the combined record reminds us how much God did in Abraham's lifetime.

To avoid discouragement in times when God seems inactive, we encourage couples to keep a record. Write down, perhaps in a journal, how you see God using your investment in others. For many years we kept ministry scrapbooks. Reviewing them helped us to appreciate how God used us for His purposes. Just like reading the life of Abraham in Genesis, your journal or scrapbook can let you see how active God is in your lives.

What parents don't have photos of their children displayed in their homes? Pictures remind parents of their victory of love and the joy of those children. When Joshua led Israel across the River Jordan to enter the Promised Land, he issued an unusual instruction. He told each tribe to take a stone for a monument. "These stones are to be a memorial to the people of Israel forever." (Joshua 4:7) The memorial reminded the people of the miracles God had done, strengthened their faith, and helped them to conquer the land. In our home, we have enlarged photos and mementos of significant God-given moments in our lives. Victories of faith and love. These reminders strengthen our faith and assure us of God's purpose in our lives.

## A Great Marriage Relationship

*Enjoy life with the woman whom you love all the days of your fleeting life which He has given to you under the sun; for this is your reward in life and in your toil in which you have labored under the sun. (Ecclesiastes 9:9)*

Couples who have children sometimes say to us, "Being married is easy for you. You don't have kids." And they are partly right. We do have more time to communicate. However, as previously explained, the amount of time we have for communication won't matter much if the communication is done poorly. The statement also minimizes the value of the natural bond a couple develops as they mutually raise their children. We don't have that natural bond. Going our own way would be more natural for us. Regardless, a strong relationship can bring great joy.

> Sometimes couples ask us, "If you could tell us just one marriage principle, the most important, what would that be?"
>
> We respond, "The single most important principle is a commitment to having a good marriage, not just a commitment to staying married." Then we add, "And the second most important principle is to develop a common plan for your marriage."

> We illustrate the plan's importance as a blueprint. "How would two carpenters building a house do if they worked from different blueprints?" Different ideas held by a husband and wife are at the root of most marriage difficulties. But developing a common plan is hard and sometimes discouraging work. That's why the commitment to having a good marriage comes first. Couples need commitment to a good marriage to develop and implement the plan.[11] (Coons, *More Than Ordinary Marriage*)

Many wonderful biblical resources teach a plan and help couples to have a successful marriage. We urge couples, especially those struggling with their relationship, to seek out these resources. We have written a mini-book, *More Than Ordinary Marriage*, that describes how to take a successful marriage to a higher level. The biblical mini-book covers topics to make a marriage joyous and productive such as serving each other, honoring, working as a team, having fun together, and even establishing healthy co-dependency. This mini-book assumes that foundational principles for a successful marriage have already been applied. But the mini-book could also give hope and commitment to couples in troubled relationships by showing how rewarding a more than ordinary marriage can be.

A more than ordinary marriage can cause others to ask, "What makes their relationship so special?" This kind of relationship can truly serve God.

> The Apostle Paul in Ephesians 5:23-32 illustrates Christ and the church using the relationship between

a husband and wife. In verse 32, he calls it a "mystery." Not all has been explained. But certainly marriages are a key part of God's purposes. Our marriage isn't just for us. A more than ordinary marriage reflects God's character. (Coons, *More Than Ordinary Marriage*)

God's character is on display in marriage. By simply having a more than ordinary marriage, couples will be teaching others by example. Most couples who came to our ministry usually hoped for more than instruction. They sought role models—couples making their relationship work, despite difficulties. And what's wrong with that? Not a thing! The Apostle Paul wrote, "Join in following my example, and observe those who walk according to the pattern you have in us." (Philippians 3:17) Being an example is a strong aspect of biblical discipleship and works especially well in the context of marriage.[12] (Coons, *More Than Ordinary Marriage*)

Some who read this have already suffered the heartbreak of a divorce. You may think, "We can't be an example in marriage. God can't use us like that." That's not true. Sometimes couples who have suffered heartbreak from the dissolution of a relationship make the best examples, if their current relationship is good. These couples don't take their relationship for granted. They know divorce can happen to them. And very frequently these previously married couples have a tremendous heart to help prevent the same tragedy from happening to others around them.

### Liking and Loving People

Will Rogers was one of the most beloved Americans of all time. He described his own popularity by, "I never met a man I didn't like." Everybody liked him because he liked them first. We can find great joy in relationships by learning to like and love people. How do you deepen your ability to like and love others? The progression of spiritual maturity in 2 Peter leads to this quality.

> *This will make possible the next step, which is for you to enjoy other people, and to like them, and finally you will grow to love them deeply. . . you will grow strong spiritually and become fruitful to our Lord Jesus Christ. (2 Peter 1:7-8, Living Bible)*

### Furry Friends

In the rough mining camps of the old American west, Mark Twain reported men living with the influence of few, if any, women. Even the women present may not have been of the best domestic influence. In this circumstance, many men lived a hard and lonely life far from their homes. Mr. Twain noted with surprise the abundance of many pampered dogs and cats. "Where there are no women," Mr. Twain concluded, "good men simply must find something to love."[13] His keen observations of human nature are timeless in their application. Pets can give us joy and an opportunity to love.

We are not suggesting that pets take the place of other people. The love of pets is in addition to love of others.

Someone has said, "You have as much love as you give away." If this is true, loving God and our neighbors and also loving pets are not in conflict. God, the source of infinite love, can surely give us extra love to share with our animal friends. And the love of pets has immeasurably enriched the lives of countless people, especially those who may live alone or have an empty spot in their hearts.

*The righteous care for the needs of their animals. (Proverbs 12:10, NIV)*

Drew: While we struggled with infertility, a part of us felt that having pets might diminish the love we would have for a prospective child. We feared that amateur psychologists might think or say, "They are trying to compensate for not having a child." We eventually came to realize that all the love we could give would still be available if God chose to bless us with a child, and that plenty of couples with children also lavish love on their pets.

Dogs and cats and even wildlife around our farm have been a big part of our lives. They add an extra dimension of unpredictability. You can joke about them without hurting their feelings. Even today our deceased pets give us joy as we recall their antics and their love for us. No matter what your challenge, you may find great comfort and joy through loving a furry friend.

## Questions for Thought

What are some ways you have found joy even in the midst of a severe challenge?

How do you remind yourself about that joy?

Has a pet ever given you comfort in a difficult time?

# MOVING *forward*

---

Our prayer for those who read this mini-book is that God will give you hope. We've looked at principles that apply to any unexpected life challenge; we've acknowledged the pain, examined unfortunate responses, and explained how we can all experience lives well lived. For us that life challenge has been childlessness. Your challenge is likely different. Regardless, the quality of our lives and the legacy we leave in our Lord is dependent on our response to the challenge.

> *"For I know the plans I have for you," declares the Lord, "plans to prosper you and not to harm you, plans to give you hope and a future." (Jeremiah 29:11, NIV)*

## The Desire of Your Heart

Kit: Occasionally people will ask me, "Kit, given your circumstances, what do you think the verse, 'He will give you the desires of your heart' in Psalm 37:4 means? Wasn't it the desire of your heart to have children? Has that desire ever gone away?" In truth, I think that if God were to give me the option to live my life over again, this time with children, I would gladly take it. But that doesn't mean He didn't keep His promise in Psalm 37:4. Because the way I see that verse is that God in His infinite wisdom gives us the best, most unselfish desires of our hearts. And more than I wanted children, I wanted to make an impact for Him. So in my case, He did give me the desire of my heart. God has enabled me to follow Him and have a life that is well invested.

## *Being Proud of the Way You Handled This*

*In all this you greatly rejoice, though now for a little while you may have had to suffer grief in all kinds of trials. These have come so that the proven genuineness of your faith—of greater worth than gold, which perishes even though refined by fire—may result in praise, glory, and honor when Jesus Christ is revealed. (1 Peter 1:6-7, NIV)*

Kit: I remember when I first felt a lump. I saw my doctor, who confirmed my worst fears. "I'm afraid this lump looks suspicious. We've made an appointment with a breast surgeon for you for tomorrow. You might also want to begin to get some information on an oncologist for the future."

My daily routine of activities ceased that day; everything changed. My new life required making decisions about my body I had never anticipated—frightening, confusing, and permanent decisions. In just five days, I had surgery. My world was completely turned upside down. Forever changed.

During that time a friend prayed for me over the phone. Her short and simple prayer made a huge impact on me and the many others with whom I have shared her words. She prayed, "Lord, help Kit to be proud of the way she handles this when it is all long over."

That prayer did two things for me. First of all, it reminded me that this would one day be long over. Her prayer gave me some much-needed perspective. And she challenged me to have victory in my circumstances. The prayer allowed me to be proud, in the good sense, of how I had handled that crisis. As Christians, we, more than anyone, can have the victory in our life journeys.

Kit endured her cancer with faith and grace. And she remains proud of the way she handled the situation. Not an ungodly pride in oneself. But rather a joyful pride that God so strengthened her. Kit's cancer was non-invasive. She has passed the five-year period to be considered a cancer survivor. Some painful challenges, like never having children, have no time limit. But life does get easier. As we have refocused our lives on God's plan for us, the pain has diminished. Will it ever completely go away? Will there ever be a time we don't twinge just a little when people ask about our children? Will we ever stop thoughts of how old our children would now be? Probably not. But our lives are far from meaningless. And we have pride in God for His work in our lives.

*In all these things we are more than conquerors through him who loved us. (Romans 8:37, NIV)*

## Redeeming the Years

The well-known parable of the talents in Matthew 25 relates to the resources God gives us with which to serve Him. No resource is more valuable than our time. The way we invest our time perhaps says more about us than anything else.

*See then that you walk circumspectly, not as fools, but as wise, Redeeming the time, because the days are evil. (Ephesians 5:15-16, KJV)*

God does many things which we do not understand. Of course, He does—He is God, perfect in wisdom, love, and power. We are only children very far from perfect in anything. At times faith must rest solidly in His character and His Word, not on our particular convictions of what He ought to do.[14] (Elliot, *My Heart for God*)

## Questions for Thought

Are you proud of the manner in which God enabled you to deal with a certain challenge? Will you tell the group?

Do you have a situation in which you aren't sure how to handle in a manner that will allow you to be proud later? Can you ask the group for ideas?

What are some ways you've been able to redeem the years in a challenging situation, or would like to?

# Bibliography

1. Coons, Kit and Drew. *More Than Ordinary Choices: Making Good Decisions*, 2018.
2. Coons, Kit and Drew. *More than Ordinary Faith: Why Does God Allow Suffering*, 2018.
3. Minirth, Frank and Les Carter. *The Anger Workbook*. (Thomas Nelson, 1993).
4. Minirth, Frank. *Happiness is a Lifestyle*. (Revell, 2005).
5. Irving, Washington. "Rip Van Winkle." (New York: P.F. Collier & Son, 1917).
6. Rainey, Dennis. *Staying Close*. (Thomas Nelson)
7. Coons, Kit and Drew. *More Than Ordinary Marriage: A Higher Level*.
8. Coons, Faith. 2.
9. Heald, Cynthia. *Becoming a Woman of Excellence*. (NavPress, 1996).
10. Gaither, Gloria. *Christianity Today*. (1992).
11. Coons, *Marriage*. 2.
12. Coons, *Marriage*. 3, 5.
13. Twain, Mark. *Roughing It*. (Sun-Times Media Group, 1872).
14. Elliot, Elisabeth. "My Heart for God." Gateway to Joy. (Vine Books, 1998).

# What is a more than ordinary life?

Each person's life is unique and special. In that sense, there is no such thing as an ordinary life. However, many people yearn for lives more special: excitement, adventure, romance, purpose, character. Our site is dedicated to the premise that any life can be more than ordinary.

At **MoreThanOrdinaryLives.com** you will find:

- inspiring stories
- entertaining novels
- ideas and resources
- free downloads

https://morethanordinarylives.com/

# Challenge Series

## by Kit and Drew Coons

### *Challenge for Two*
Book One

A series of difficult circumstances have forced Dave and Katie Parker into early retirement. Searching for new life and purpose, the Parkers take a wintertime job house sitting an old Victorian mansion. The picturesque river town in southeastern Minnesota is far from the climate and culture of their home near the Alabama Gulf Coast.

But dark secrets sleep in the mansion. A criminal network has ruthlessly intimidated the community since the timber baron era of the 19th century. Residents have been conditioned to look the other way.

The Parkers' questions about local history and clues they discover in the mansion bring an evil past to light and create division in the small community. While some fear the consequences of digging up the truth, others want freedom from crime and justice for victims. Faced with personal threats, the Parkers must decide how to respond for themselves and for the good of the community.

## *Challenge Down Under*
### Book Two

Dave and Katie Parker's only son, Jeremy, is getting married in Australia. In spite of initial reservations, the Parkers discover that Denyse is perfect for Jeremy and that she's the daughter they've always wanted. But she brings with her a colorful and largely dysfunctional Aussie family. Again Dave and Katie are fish out of water as they try to relate to a boisterous clan in a culture very different from their home in South Alabama.

After the wedding, Denyse feels heartbroken that her younger brother, Trevor, did not attend. Details emerge that lead Denyse to believe her brother may be in trouble. Impressed by his parents' sleuthing experience in Minnesota, Jeremy volunteers them to locate Trevor. Their search leads them on an adventure through Australia and New Zealand.

Unfortunately, others are also searching for Trevor, with far more sinister intentions. With a talent for irresponsible chicanery inherited from his family, Trevor has left a trail of trouble in his wake and has been forced into servitude. Can Dave and Katie locate him in time?

## *Challenge in Mobile*
## Book Three

Dave and Katie Parker regret that their only child Jeremy, his wife Denyse, and their infant daughter live on the opposite side of the world. Unexpectedly, Jeremy calls to ask his father's help finding an accounting job in the US. Katie urges Dave to do whatever is necessary to find a job for Jeremy near Mobile. Dave's former accounting firm has floundered since his departure. The Parkers risk their financial security by purchasing full ownership of the struggling firm to make a place for Jeremy.

Denyse finds South Alabama fascinating compared to her native Australia. She quickly resumes her passion for teaching inner-city teenagers. Invited by Katie, other colorful guests arrive from Australia and Minnesota to experience Gulf Coast culture. Aided by their guests, Dave and Katie examine their faith after Katie receives discouraging news from her doctors.

Political, financial, and racial tensions have been building in Mobile. Bewildering financial expenditures of a client create suspicions of criminal activity. Denyse hears disturbing rumors from her students. A hurricane from the Gulf of Mexico exacerbates the community's tensions. Dave and Katie are pulled into a crisis that requires them to rise to a new level of more than ordinary.

# More from Kit and Drew Coons

## The Ambassadors

Two genetically engineered beings unexpectedly arrive on Earth. Unlike most extraterrestrials depicted in science fiction, the pair is attractive, personable, and telegenic—the perfect talk show guests. They have come to Earth as ambassadors bringing an offer of partnership in a confederation of civilizations. Technological advances are offered as part of the partnership. But humans must learn to cooperate among themselves to join.

Molly, a young reporter, and Paul, a NASA scientist, have each suffered personal tragedy and carry emotional baggage. They are asked to tutor the ambassadors in human ways and to guide them on a worldwide goodwill tour. Molly and Paul observe as the extraterrestrials commit faux pas while experiencing human culture. They struggle trying to define a romance and partnership while dealing with burdens of the past.

However, mankind finds implementing actual change difficult. Clashing value systems and conflicts among subgroups of humanity erupt. Inevitably, rather than face difficult choices, fear-mongers in the media start to blame the messengers. Then an uncontrolled biological weapon previously created by a rogue country tips the world into chaos. Molly, Paul, and the others must face complex moral decisions about what being human means and the future of mankind.

## MINI SERIES

**More Than Ordinary Challenges—**
Dealing with the Unexpected

**More Than Ordinary Marriage—**
A Higher Level

**More Than Ordinary Faith—**
Why Does God Allow Suffering?

**More Than Ordinary Wisdom—**
Stories of Faith and Folly

**More Than Ordinary Abundance—**
From Kit's Heart

**More Than Ordinary Choices—**
Making Good Decisions

Visit **https://morethanordinarylives.com/**
for more information.

# About the Authors

Kit and Drew Coons met while Christian missionaries in Africa in 1980. As humorous speakers specializing in strengthening relationships, they have taught in every part of the US and in thirty-nine other countries. For two years, the Coonses lived and served in New Zealand and Australia. They are keen cultural observers and incorporate their many adventures into their writing. Kit and Drew are unique in that they speak and write as a team.

Made in the USA
Middletown, DE
08 April 2019